OLD BIG 'EAD

OLD

BIG 'EAD

THE WIT AND WISDOM OF
BRIAN CLOUGH

Compiled by Duncan Hamilton

Aurum

First published in 2009 by Aurum Press Ltd
7 Greenland Street, London NW1 0ND
www.aurumpress.co.uk

Compilation copyright © 2009 Duncan Hamilton

A catalogue record for this book is available from the British Library.

ISBN 978 1 84513 476 1

10 9 8 7 6 5 4 3 2 1
2013 2012 2011 2010 2009

Designed by Roger Hammond
Printed and bound in Great Britain by MPG Books, Bodmin,
Cornwall

CONTENTS

OLD BIG "EAD

INTRODUCTION

Brian Clough knew how to work the levers and pulleys of the media better than any football manager I've ever known. The proof of it exists in the book you're holding.

No one else in the 'trade' (which is how Brian frequently described his job) justifies having his thoughts bound between hard covers. That's because no one ever had more of them, or could articulate an argument as cogently or as compellingly as he could. None of his contemporaries were as consistently quotable. As for those who have trod the managerial path since his retirement . . . well, let's just say football has changed. In the stagey protocol of the Premiership press conference – often banal, stiff and predictable occasions – the questions often carry a higher value than the answers, which lean towards the anodyne. Even when the answers are worth writing down and printing, the words usually don't linger or

OLD BIG "EAD

stay hot in the mind for long. If only Brian was still around . . .

He diligently made it his business to understand the mechanics of the press – print and broadcast – and did so specifically so he could benefit from that knowledge. What he gave in return was good copy. He was football's Mr Punch, always putting on a show.

The glib assumption, usually espoused by people who didn't know him, is that Brian was foremost a skillful self-publicist. But long before he became a manager in 1965, he had the foresight and nous to reach, independently, two important conclusions. First, that he could use the media the way a fairground barker uses a loud-hailer to whip up a crowd. If he talked well and loudly enough on the back pages, he could chastise his players, rouse supporters, intimidate the opposition, rebuke authority (especially the Football Association) and burnish his own image; sometimes all at once. Second, that he was perfectly placed to take advantage of the television age. He was young and handsome and prepared to say in public what others would only whisper in private. The camera loved him.

'*Talking is easy,*' he once said. '*If I have an opinion, there's nowt wrong with sharing it. All I have to do is open my mouth and say it.*'

Three of his most famous quotes girdle the eight-foot high statue erected in his honour near Nottingham's Old Market Square. You can probably recite them verbatim.

If God had wanted us to play football in the clouds, He'd have put grass up there.

We talk about it for twenty minutes and then we decide I was right.

I wouldn't say I was the best manager in the business. But I was in the top one.

This is the quintessential Brian. The first emphasises his approach to football. The second highlights his uncompromising approach to club discipline. The third cheekily reflects how he saw himself. That well judged selection nonetheless amounts to no more than the narrow tip of a vast, mountainous heap of

OLD BIG "EAD

'Cloughisms' that informed, entertained or – quite frequently – got him into trouble. Each quote is the equivalent of a snapshot, catching him for a split second in a slightly different pose. Strung together and seen as a whole, the quotes reveal glimpses of his personality and upbringing as well as mapping the landscape of his life: his prejudices and foibles, his philosophy and aesthetic approach to the game, his peaks and troughs as both player and manager. For me, what each one demonstrates is the complexity and contradictory nature of his character. He could be infuriatingly brusque and bitter, compassionate and tender, provocative and funny; so funny, in fact, that he could make me weep convulsively.

During my time as a sports reporter for the *Nottingham Evening Post* I was ostensibly tasked with covering Nottingham Forest. In reality, I was attached to Brian rather than to the team. He was the source of 99 per cent of my stories.

I always went to see him with an amalgam of hope and trepidation. What mood would he be in? Which Brian would turn up? The curt, bombastic Brian or the emollient and considerate one? How long would he make me wait? Five minutes or five and a half hours? Sitting on a chair in the corridor outside his office, I felt like – and resembled – one of Beckett's forlorn tramps waiting for Godot. But, however long this torturous process took, I don't remember leaving without a story.

Often he gave me the complete structure too, as if he'd been trained to write on a sports desk himself. '*I've got an intro for you*,' he'd say and then dictate it before I'd found my pen and notebook. He'd soon be in full flow, often discussing things only tangentially linked to the central subject, before ending with a flourish. '*That's your out*,' he'd say, meaning the final paragraph or punch-line.

Belatedly I realised that he sometimes rehearsed in his own mind what to say beforehand – to players as well as to journalists

OLD BIG "EAD

– far more often than he ever let on. But his theatrical tendencies made it seem as though the 'angle' for a piece had only just occurred to him.

I can see and hear him now. His hands are behind his head, his feet resting on the corner of his cluttered desk. He's leaning back in his chair. *'You'll miss me when I go,'* he's saying. *''Cos you'll have nowt interesting to put in that rag of yours.'*

And, of course, he was right.

BRIAN'S EARLY LIFE AND PLAYING CAREER

Born:
21 March 1935
Player record:
Middlesbrough (1955-61): 197 goals in 213 games
Sunderland (1961-64): 54 goals in 61 games

Brian was born in a council house in Middlesbrough, the fifth of eight children. '*We kicked a ball around for hours. We were still at it late at night when we couldn't see the ball, the makeshift posts or one another,*' he once said, adding later that: '*There were always about six pairs of boots hanging behind the coalhouse door.*' His father Joe worked in a sweet factory. '*We'd get all the misshapen sweets that couldn't be sold in shops,*' he said. His mother Sarah was an indefatigable housewife, always cooking and cleaning and bringing up her children to '*behave properly and be considerate to others*'.

OLD BIG "EAD

His playing career effectively ended on Boxing Day, 1962. On a frosty pitch he collided with Bury goalkeeper Chris Harker and damaged his cruciate ligaments. He never properly recovered and made only another three appearances before his premature retirement.

'The most vivid Christmas of all was the year I got the turkey leg. You see, I had a long wait for it. There were eight in the family and only two legs on the turkey.' 1985

'In the North East, the front step of your house was important. It had to be so spotless that you could have eaten your Sunday dinner off it. Ours was – it was the best in the street. It gave our mam a great deal of pride.' 1983

'When I was a bairn, in the era of baggy shorts, growing up in the North East meant that you were raised on stories of great centre forwards.' 1981

'My dad was a football fanatic and he worked in a sweet factory. What else does a boy need?' 1976

OLD BIG 'EAD

'Wilf Mannion was my hero. It was as if he'd walked straight out of the cinema screen. In Middlesbrough, he was like a movie star. Hollywood on our streets.' 1976

'I was taught the importance of clean shoes. Mind you, I had to polish them hard. I wore the toes out of most of them kicking a ball around.' 1972

'At school I was a failure. I suppose I was thick ... I cried when I failed my 11-plus.' 1972

'We used to sleep three to a bed. There was me, our Bill and our Gerald. We were never cold.' 1990

'At first Middlesbrough thought I was crap – too mouthy, too awkward. The club used that as an excuse not to see what I could do on the pitch.' 1989

'We were beaten 6-3 at Charlton once. I got the three. On the way home I said: "If we score five next week, do you think we'll get a point?" ... That sort of thing didn't go down well with centre halves.' 2000

'Alan Brown influenced me because I respected him so much. And he scared me half to death. You didn't want to be on the end of one of his bollockings. The first thing he ever said to me was: "You may have heard that I'm a bastard ... well, they're right." And yes, he could be. But he was a brilliant one.'

On his mentor Alan Brown, manager of Sunderland 1984

OLD BIG "EAD

'I always remember trying to get up when the ball broke free. I tried to crawl after it, but I couldn't move ... The Bury centre-half Bob Stokoe was shouting at me: "Get up ... there's nothing wrong with you."'

On the injury which effectively ended his playing career 1968

'I not only did my knee, I banged my head. A lot of people have put it down to the way I've behaved for the last ten years.'

Making light of his damaged knee 1977

'The best thing I ever did in my life. Oh, was I lucky.'

On marrying his wife Barbara 1990

'He was so wrong because I was a better player than the bloke he took. He was a lad called Derek Kevan and he couldn't play at all compared to my ability.'

On Walter Winterbottom's decision to leave him out of the 1958 World Cup squad 1981

'Publicity is not my strong suit. Some footballers like to
see their name constantly in the headlines. I don't.'

He protests too much 1958

'I am very happy to have scored 250 League goals
faster than anyone else.'

Typical modesty about his goal-scoring record 1976

'It certainly wasn't luck, and I don't mean that
conceitedly 'cause you can't get lucky 40 times a year.
You can get lucky five times, but not 40.'

On the fact he regularly scored 40 goals a season 2001

OLD BIG "EAD

BRIAN ON
HARTLEPOOL UNITED

October, 1965

At just 29, Brian became a manager, with Peter Taylor as his assistant. He described taking over at Hartlepool as like '*dropping off the end of the world*'. The club were hopelessly impecunious, and nearly always finished near the bottom of the Fourth Division. His first chairman Ernest Ord used to ring his office at 4.55pm each day just to make sure '*I hadn't scarpered home early*'. He once told Brian he would be dealing with the club's publicity. '*He thought he was managing Hollywood, not Hartlepool,*' he said. '*But we were so obscure we were lucky to get a mention in the classified results.*'

OLD BIG "EAD

'It won't be a little place for very long ... I know I am better than the 500 or so managers who have been sacked since the War. If they had known anything about the game, they wouldn't have lost their jobs.'
On taking over 1965

'Age doesn't count. It's what you know about football that matters.'
Dismissing his age as irrelevant 1965

'I didn't talk him into coming. I just showed him some pound notes. Two hundred, actually.'
On persuading Peter Taylor to join him 1990

'He threatened to sack me at least 43 times a week.'
On his first chairman, Ernest Ord 1989

'I got the sack at Hartlepool – and refused to go. The bloke who told me to clear off was called Ernest Ord ... we had more rows than Jack Duckworth and his missus in Coronation Street. I stayed – and got rid of him.' 1989

'He was the shortest fella I've ever met. So small that when he got behind the wheel of his Rolls Royce, you'd have thought no one was driving it.'
On Ord again 1989

'I cut the grass and cleaned the drains and even mopped the dressing room floor ... We travelled jammed in our own private cars. Fifteen of us went to Barnsley once for £22 – petrol, meals, the lot.'
Life at Harlepool 1969

OLD BIG 'EAD

BRIAN ON DERBY COUNTY

May, 1967

Hartlepool finished eighth in the season before Brian and Peter Taylor – on the recommendation of Len Shackleton, a seminal figure in North East football – moved to Derby, then in the Second Division. Derby won the Division Two title in 1969, the League Championship in 1972 and reached the European Cup semi-finals in 1973. Brian resigned in the autumn of 1973 after a row with chairman Sam Longson and the board. Even a players' revolt – and unequivocal support from the terraces – couldn't re-instate him. It taught Brian a lesson. '*Never resign*,' he said. His decision to do so was, he said, the consequence of having '*too much time to think – and not enough brain to think with*.'

OLD BIG "EAD

'Well, we're not as good as some as far as skill is concerned. But we'll beat most of them because they destroy themselves through lack of discipline, preparation, attitude, self-control and things like that.'
His belief that Derby could survive in the First Division 1969

'When I first came to Derby, the fans used to say: "He's a cocky bugger." But we started winning things and they put up with me.' 1972

'We used to have 'em in on Saturday morning and say: "Gentlemen, cut out your night-clubbing, cut out opening garages, cut out your birding, boozing and smoking. We are closing ranks." We always used to emerge stronger.'
On recovering from a poor run of results at Derby 1981

'We haven't got a chance of the title.'
Less than a month before Derby won it 1972

'This is one of the miracles of the century. Our triumph proves there is hope for all the little people of the world.'

After winning the title 1972

'I'm frightened about winning the championship. I'm frightened about the responsibilities involved in being champions, the people who are going to feel let down if things don't go as we want.'

On the sense of expectation at the start of the following season 1972

'No cheating bastards will I talk to;
I will not talk to any cheating bastards.'

Refusing to speak to the Italian press after Juventus beat Derby in Turin in the 1973 European Cup semi-finals. He maintained the referee had been bribed. 1973

OLD BIG "EAD

'Taylor began telling the board that the team was so good that even Longson could manage it. And Longson began to believe it.'

On the reasons for the rift with the board that led to his resignation 1989

'My feelings now are of complete and utter pity for Derby County.'

After his resignation 1973

'There have been months of sleepless nights. I know Peter hasn't been sleeping and he knows I haven't been sleeping because we have had to telephone each other to talk about our problems at ridiculous hours.'

On the stress that decision caused 1973

'I dropped the worst clanger of my career by walking out on Derby. It was an absolute tragedy. I quit without a penny when I should have stayed to fight the blokes on the board who wanted me out.' 1989

'You start off in the game thinking you're indispensable. It never occurred to me that I wasn't indispensable at Derby, for example. I even told them so. I soon found out I was talking crap. There's always someone who can sit in your chair.'1993

'I was dafter than I am now. And brasher. And louder. And less experienced.'
Why he quit 1990

OLD BIG "EAD

'If I hadn't cleared off, if things had been different, Liverpool wouldn't have won all those trophies – Derby would have got there first.'

His claim that Derby would have outdone Liverpool in the 1970s and 80s 1989

'You must convince players that you are the greatest thing they have ever come into contact with. If you say Father Christmas really exists, they have to believe it.'

A message to his successor Dave Mackay 1973

'She came up with one of the wisest and most sensible statements I've ever heard. "If you go back," she said, "you'd be nuts."'

Not accepting Derby's offer to return in 1977, on the advice of his wife Barbara 1989

'I don't know why it is that clubs always want me when I am in work.'

After Derby had tried to take him from Forest 1977

'I'm sick and tired of being asked whether Derby hold a special place in my heart. They don't.' 1983

'Some of my heart, wherever I have wandered, was in Derby ... I wish I'd never left. It was the best job I ever had ... It's like your first girlfriend. You don't forget, do you?'

On his love for Derby 2002

OLD BIG 'EAD

BRIAN ON BRIGHTON AND HOVE ALBION

November, 1973

Out of work, Brian swiftly moved to Third Division Brighton with Peter Taylor. '*We were starting again*,' he said. It proved an impossible task to revive them. Having begun his career there with the provocative '*Of course, I'm bigger than Brighton!*', he soon found that he missed the starry glamour of the First Division and disliked travelling to and from the South Coast. Still living in Derby and regularly commuting, he said: '*I'd get through London and then see a sign that read: Brighton 50 miles. My heart always sank.*'

OLD BIG "EAD

'If the players are apprehensive about me, they will have to get over it. I am here for a long time. They will have to shoot me to get me out.' 1973

'All I knew about Brighton was that it had a pier.'
On his ignorance of the club 1990

'I couldn't accept that I swapped the England centre half and six internationals for a bunch of players who couldn't put their boots on the right feet. It was like asking Lester Piggott to win the Derby on a Skegness donkey – and then telling him he was rubbish when he didn't do it.'

The reality of the job 1990

'My young lad Nigel would insist on going to school with a Brighton bag. They gave him hell.'
On the consequences of bad results 1977

'We spent an absolute fortune, got knocked out of the FA Cup by an amateur side and all we managed to do was finish fourth from bottom. That was my one and only period of self doubt.' 1990

'I am going to America for the big fight because I have missed the big time.'
Why he flew to New York to watch Muhammad Ali versus Joe Frazier while still manager of Brighton 1974

'Brighton and I are having an affair and we'll never be right for one another until the day we are married.'
On his struggle for results 1974

'I cannot adapt to Third Division football.'
Facing up to his inevitable departure 1974

OLD BIG "EAD

'I didn't make a mistake in going to Brighton. I just went there for the wrong reasons.' 1974

'My kids went through the purgatory of living in a football kingdom where I was the King who had been deposed.'
Life at Brighton 1978

BRIAN ON LEEDS UNITED

July, 1974

During the previous seven years, Brian perpetually criticised Leeds and their manager Don Revie. '*I didn't like the way they played football*,' he said. When Revie won the League title for the second time in 1974 and became England manager, the Leeds board inexplicably chose Brian to replace him. Of competing against Revie, he admitted: '*Only by doing something he hasn't, can I exceed him. I've got to win the European Cup.*' What followed were rows, recriminations, only four League points from a possible 12 and, finally, the sack after only 44 days. Brian claimed the club had to pay him six-figure compensation. It changed the rest of his football life.

OLD BIG "EAD

'Name your price. You can have whatever you want to come up here and help me. It's too much for one.'

To Peter Taylor, who declined to join him at Elland Road 1974

'I can warn the superstitious Leeds stars of this: the new boss will never join their pre-match Bingo sessions. I will give them my last breath, my last penny, but I absolutely refuse to play Bingo.'

His decision to change Leeds' pre-match routine 1974

'Chuck your medals on the table – 'cos you won 'em by cheating.'

His first team meeting at Leeds United 1974

'The players have more meetings than the union at Ford.'

On dressing room opposition to his methods 1974

'By next April, whether we win anything or not, I will have proved to Billy Bremner that I'm as good a manager as Don Revie – or better.' 1974

'I was prepared to show the white flag of truce. He shot me down while I was still fifty yards away ... He made me feel like an intruder, a gatecrasher at a New Year's Eve party. Sometimes I don't think he was aware of how he made me feel.'

On his relationship with Bremner 1974

'It was 44 days of tension, conflict and unpleasantness ... and I wasn't there long enough to find out where to park the car.' 1990

OLD BIG 'EAD

'I under-estimated the depth of feeling against me and ... I tried to change everything at Leeds much too quickly.'

On why he was sacked 1978

'If the club had stayed loyal, and shown a bit of courage, I'd have given them the one thing Don Revie didn't get his hands on – the European Cup.' 1990

'When the hurt of being out of work had gone, I wanted to kiss the Leeds board, not strangle them. I was the luckiest man alive 'cos I won the pools without filling in the coupon ... I was the richest bloke in the dole queue. I could have drunk champagne instead of Tizer, eaten caviar rather than fish and chips. All thanks to Leeds.'

On receiving what he claimed was £100,000 compensation from Leeds 1990

'I remember that I took my cheque straight to the bank. If anyone was that shallow and stupid to sack me after 44 days, I didn't trust them.' 1989

'I have been to the two extremes in football. I have been to the very top and I've got the sack.' 1975

OLD BIG 'EAD

BRIAN ON
NOTTINGHAM FOREST

January, 1975 – May, 1993

After leaving Leeds, Brian said immediately: *'I'm thick enough to believe I'll get back into football.'* Asked why he'd returned to the game, he replied: *'At 39, I am too young to retire.'*

A job that began on a grey winter's morning was to last more than 18 years. During it, Nottingham Forest won one League Championship, two European Cups, four League Cups (in various guises) and the admiration of everyone who saw them play fluently and with a high-minded moral obligation to pass the ball on the floor. *'We played the game the way it ought to be played,'* he said. *'Our passes brushed the grass.'*

OLD BIG 'EAD

'I've left the human race and rejoined the rat race.'

On returning to football after four months away 1975

'There is only one thing in the club's favour. It has got me.'

On Forest's parlous mid-table position in the old Second Division 1975

'We couldn't have beaten a team from *Come Dancing*.'

On the Forest team he took over 1989

'When I started at Nottingham Forest, there was an empty row of seats at the back of the box – 'cos some idiots were spitting at the committee.' 1990

'The people who said the Anglo-Scottish Cup was nothing were crackers. It was something to us ... It provided us with a cup, and players who hadn't won anything got a medal. They tasted the champagne ... and they liked it.'

Looking back on winning the club's first trophy (in 1976) since the FA Cup of 1959 1981

'Gentlemen, no swearing please – Brian'

The sign he had erected in front of the Trent End to curtail bad language 1977

'I knew it would be bad at Forest. I just didn't know how awful. Our training ground was about as attractive as Siberia in mid-winter without your coat on, our training kit looked like something you got from the Oxfam shop. We barely had a player in the first team who I thought could play ... I even had to teach one of them how to take a throw in. I also had to teach them to dress smartly, take their hands out of their pockets and stop slouching.'

On his first season at Forest 1981

OLD BIG "EAD

'I thought we'd do it before Peter arrived. The second he walked through the door, I knew it.'

On promotion to the First Division after Peter Taylor rejoined him in the summer of 1976 1981

'We are the Wembley virgins.'

Description of his team before the 1978 League Cup final against Liverpool. Forest won the replay at Old Trafford 1-0.

'It's not meant to be disparaging, but I felt more satisfaction after clinching it at Derby. Perhaps it was because it was the first time ... I don't know.'

On winning the 1977-78 championship with Forest 1981

'Not as good as the Derby side and not as close knit.'

Comparing Forest to Derby's championship sides 1990

'We treat our European matches like seaside holidays, a break from the factory floor of the Football League. We enjoy ourselves, even though we pack our boots rather than a bucket and spade.'

On the way to winning the European Cup 1979

'If you're a club manager – and only a club manager – the way you can partly play at being an international one is to win the European Cup. All hopes had gone for me and the England job by then [1979]. If I wasn't getting it in 1977, I was never getting it. All I had left was the European Cup. Winning it was my equivalent of the World Cup.'

On the importance of Forest's European Cup wins to him 1981

'The Red Cross sent us parcels at Christmas ... I think the board probably thought about sacking me at least once a week.'

On Forest's parlous financial position in the early 1980s, when the club's glory years began to fade 1990

OLD BIG "EAD

'We took one sugar in our tea instead of two, we used margarine rather than butter, and we all drank Tizer instead of Scotch because we got thruppence back on the empty bottle.'

On scraping together the pennies in those hard-pressed days 1990

'Listen, our lot are so young most of 'em still believe in Father Christmas. I haven't the heart to tell them the truth.'

On the average age of Forest's team 1984

'Our problem isn't injury – it's acne.'

Dwelling again on the youthfulness of his players 1984

'My action, no matter how misguided, was taken with the right motives. I was concerned about a possible confrontation between our supporters and the other lot ... If I catch spectators on my pitch in future, I know exactly what I'll do. They'll get another clip around the earhole. I hit five pitch invaders – and I would have got all 300 if I could.'

On striking fans who came on to the pitch after a Littlewoods Cup tie against QPR 1989

'I stuck the Cup on the TV and watched a replay with my family. I kept it there for two days, actually. Sometimes you wake up and think whether you've dreamt something. I went into our lounge and knew I hadn't.'

After Forest's Littlewoods Cup win at Wembley over Luton 1989

'It doesn't affect me. Other people want to win it for me more than I want to win it.'

On the FA Cup 1990

OLD BIG "EAD

'The FA Cup? A perk. A lovely day out. It's that gala occasion when thousands of people who never watch football throughout the year suddenly turn up in the best seats and the biggest hats.'

Before the 1991 FA Cup final against Tottenham

'Whoever succeeds me at Forest will upset me if he does less than I have done. I want him to win more.' 1988

'No one will ever do what I did at Nottingham Forest. Now that's something to keep you warm at night.' 1994

BRIAN ON ENGLAND

Brian was always the 'People's Choice' as England manager, a fact the Football Association ignored for expediency's sake. After his interview at Lancaster Gate in 1977, he did think, albeit very briefly, that he might have won the FA over. In retrospect he knew it had been wishful thinking. At the time, he thought: '*The job's mine. I didn't so much walk out of the room as float. I was absolutely brilliant.*' With hindsight, he admitted: '*I didn't legislate for the fact that when the FA get into their stride they make the Mafia look like kindergarten material.*' The FA threw him a conciliatory bone. He briefly took charge of the England Youth team.

OLD BIG "EAD

'I think they had a sneaking suspicion that I would try to run the FA. They were shrewd and absolutely right. I'd have taken over everything.' 1985

'I was never going to get that job. But when the FA saw I wasn't the awful, snarling spitting bombastic bloke they'd imagined, I took them by utter surprise.'
On his interview 1984

'I was just too risky. The FA wanted Ron Greenwood – good guy, safe but boring. They wanted the whole thing kept cosy. They wanted to take their wives on overseas trips, travelling first class and staying in nice hotels where cocktails were served on the veranda. They wanted to wear the England badge on their blazer. Bugger the World Cup.'
Why he didn't get the job 1982

'I'd have tried not to give them the time of day.'
On the FA councillors 1985

'I might have lasted less than 44 days.'
After being asked whether he'd have been a success with England 1990

'If the post of England manager had been filled on the basis of outstanding achievement, then Ron Greenwood would not have had a smell.' 1982

'If Taylor and I had got that job, we'd have won the bloody thing.'
On England in the 1982 World Cup finals

'The chance of England disappeared four years ago. I then resigned myself to never getting the job and withdrawing from all future races.' 1981

OLD BIG "EAD

'Barbara said I talked myself out of the England manager's job. I think she may be right.' 1990

'I don't know who you are and I don't know who gave you permission to come in here. But fuck off.'

To the England team doctor, who unwisely entered the dressing room with a plate of half time oranges during an England Youth international 1978

'England managers seem to forget the principles of good management as soon as they get the job. Don Revie did. So did Ron Greenwood. That's why I'd move the FA to Doncaster if I ever became England boss. I would be as far away from London as I could, then I wouldn't have the so-called experts giving me advice every ten minutes.' 1983

'I wish Robson could have had a friend who would have draped an arm around his shoulders and taken him to one side and said: "Don't take it, pal. Stay at Ipswich. Put your wife and family foremost. Don't be a fool. The grass is greenest right here."'

On Bobby Robson's decision to leave Ipswich and become England manager 1984

'I'm fed up with Bobby Robson pointing at his grey hairs and saying that the England manager's job has aged him 10 years. If he doesn't like it, why doesn't he go back to his orchard in Ipswich?' 1988

'I could manage England part-time and still walk the dog.'

After his retirement 1993

'At last England have appointed a manager who speaks better English than the players.'

On the appointment of Sweden's Sven Goran Eriksson 2001

OLD BIG "EAD

'I might be an old codger now and slightly past my best as a gaffer, but the FA know I'll keep my trousers on.'

In the aftermath of allegations about Sven Goran Eriksson's personal life 2004

'I just happen to think I'd have been brilliant.'

On whether he'd have made a good England manager 1993

Although the Football Association were afraid of Brian, there were other countries – significantly Wales, the Republic of Ireland and, improbably, Iran in the early 1970s – who flirted with him during his career. Brian listened to their blandishments and frequently used their courtship to improve his own contract at Nottingham Forest.

'I'm telling you, there wouldn't have been more of an outcry if the Welsh FA had dug up Dr Crippen and given him the chance of going to the next World Cup.'
On the reaction to the Welsh FA's decision to offer him the job as national team manager 1988

'Becoming Welsh manager is a dream come true because I need to sample senior international football before my career ends. Now I can discover whether my methods work on the world stage.' 1988

OLD BIG "EAD

'I didn't have to talk money with them. I could buy the bloody Welsh FA ... I told them that if they were hard up they needn't hire a coach for matches. I'd use my company car. It's a big Mercedes and I'd get most of their squad in it.' 1988

'They were wrong, you know, I could have done both jobs.'
On the Forest board's decision not allow him to take the Welsh job part-time 1988

'I know there wouldn't be any problems getting across to Dublin. It's just a straight walk across the Irish Sea for me.'
On being linked with the Republic of Ireland manager's job

'I want to be manager of Scotland. If I thought for one second the Scottish Football Association would give me the chance, I'd grab it.' 1986

BRIAN ON PETER TAYLOR

Clough and Taylor: It was like a marriage, and at times the two of them acted like a married couple – spurring one another on, bickering occasionally and falling out. What kept them together for so long? *'The main thing we've got in common is that we like the same things,'* said Brian. What drove them apart? Peter's signing of John Roberston on FA Cup final day, 1983, without informing Brian first. How much did Brian miss Peter after their friendship broke apart? *'He was the only bloke who made me laugh,'* Brian said.

OLD BIG "EAD

'Pete was the only bloke who could stick an arm around my shoulder and tell me – straightforwardly, mate to mate – that I was wrong or right or to just shut up and get on with the job. When I rang him to say I'd got Hartlepool, and did he fancy it, we'd barely spoken for four years. We were football people and, like the circus, sometimes you have to travel to scrape a living. But I knew I needed him. I knew we were right together.' 1991

'It was as if he could read minds. He'd nudge me and say: "So and so needs picking up – can't you see the droop of his shoulders?" Or: "That bloke is too cocky by half. He needs yanking down a peg or two."' 1991

'We were the first to introduce the two-man job. Now everybody's copied it. And nobody needed a steadying influence more than I did. When I wanted to leap to my feet and fight somebody or tell them to fuck off, Taylor would say: "Hang on, I'll deal with this."' 1988

'Without him, my job would be impossible.' 1966

'I object to the word 'assistant' when he is talked about. He's my partner – the only man in football who can spend big money without the manager's sanction.' 1969

'I'm the shop window – he's the goods at the back.' 1971

'We were arrogant at the bottom and we are arrogant at the top – that's consistency.' 1979

'He wouldn't have shifted a copy without my mug on the front, my name alongside it and my thoughts on every page.'

Incandescent that Taylor had written a book – *With Clough, by Taylor* – without telling him about it 1980

OLD BIG "EAD

'He said: "We've shot it, haven't we?" I said: "No, you have!" ... But when he sat in his office and told me he wanted to get out of the game, I cried.'

When Taylor broke the news of his retirement 1982

'I would not dream of having anyone else to work alongside me as close as Peter did. I couldn't find anyone as good for a start.'

Asked whether he would ever again appoint an assistant manager 1982

'I would have thought that the logical thing to do, after Peter decided retirement wasn't for him, would have been to come back to Forest. The door was still open – and still is. But if he wants a lift from his home to the Baseball Ground, he can have one.'

On Taylor's decision to manage Derby six months later 1982

'One call. Two lines in a letter.
That's all it needed.'

**His lament after Taylor signed John Robertson for Derby
without telling him** 1983

'If I saw him on the A52 thumbing a lift, I'd run him
down. He's lost the one friend he had in the world.
And that's me ... In my book, the man is a rattlesnake.'
His angry response to it 1983

'They wouldn't have come through the front door
unless they saw my mug. There was a myth here that
someone else was doing it, but I was the one who
wheeled and dealed for players.'
On who was the dominant partner in the transfer market 1984

OLD BIG "EAD

'What a waste. All those years when we could have been sitting together having a beer. All of those years when he could have come as an honoured guest to watch us play. All those years without the laughter he was capable of providing.'

On Taylor's premature death in October 1990 and the feud which broke their relationship 1990

'My son Nigel, the one who plays centre forward for me at Nottingham Forest, asked me recently if I had any regrets. It was when Peter Taylor had died. I told my son: "He should have seen you play at Wembley the last couple of times."' 1990

'No. Easy. Barbara said, "we're going." Peter Taylor had carried my children on his back.'

Asked whether it had been a difficult decision to attend Peter Taylor's funeral 1992

BRIAN ON MANAGERS

Brian never subscribed to Bill Shankly's exaggerated belief that football was more important than life and death. He nonetheless respected and liked Shankly, regarding him unequivocally as the archetypal *'football man'*. He also had an empathy with managers who shared his aesthetic beliefs about how the game ought to be played. *'Jim Smith paid me one of the biggest compliments I've ever got,'* he said. *'He told me that whenever he was feeling low, he'd watch a video of one of our matches because we played football the way it ought to be played.'*

OLD BIG "EAD

'Sir Alf has picked the wrong teams. That's all there is to the argument.'

On Sir Alf Ramsey's failure to qualify for the World Cup finals 1973

'I remember once taking the trouble on a Sunday morning to find Alf's telephone number in Ipswich to ring him and let him know that a Derby player was unfit. "Thank you. But you could have rung me tomorrow" ... Well, I will never waste my time again on a Sunday for Sir Alf Ramsey.' 1972

'We have to deal with these people. But Bill Shankly wouldn't have let them within fifty miles of Anfield. Bill would have gone barmy if he had to say to a player: "Do you want to come to Liverpool?" and the player had said: "I want to talk to my agent." Bill would have hit him.'

On agents and his respect for Bill Shankly 1980

'Bill Shankly talked more sense about football than the rest of the Football League put together. Mind you, I'm excluding myself from that assessment.' 1974

'Sir Matt Busby was a great manager, but he made one mistake in the boardroom. When Manchester United were looking for a manager, he didn't pick up a phone and call the one man who could have walked the job. Me.'

1975

'Bill Nicholson used to say that a pat on the back isn't too far from a kick up the arse. He was right.'
On Spurs' double-winning boss 1982

OLD BIG 'EAD

'I once asked Peter Taylor why people failed in football management. Men like Billy Wright, who must have known the game from A to Z. Those who fail are the ones who can't impart their knowledge to us. Billy Wright couldn't have talked football to my daughter Elizabeth.' 1988

'You know that little smile he has got, that pleasant manner? Well, he hates losing worse than me. I underestimated him, good old dear Bob. He had me sitting on a skip drinking Newcastle Brown Ale when he took over. "Come in and have a drink," he said. "Nice to see you Brian." They beat us. I haven't sat on that skip since.'

On Liverpool's Bob Paisley 1981

'When they gave Kenny [Dalglish] the Anfield manager's job, he didn't just win the pools – he made off with the Crown Jewels.'

On the good fortune of being manager of Liverpool 1987

'They caress a football the way I dreamt of caressing Marilyn Monroe ... Their speed of thought and movement are incredible and they are the supreme essence of skill. Wenger is one of the great managers. However, with respect, we were Nottingham Forest and they are Arsenal.'

After Arsenal overtook Forest's run of 42 unbeaten League matches 2004

'I hate to mention him because he's a very talented man and I don't like him ... I don't like the way he goes about football either.'

On Don Revie 1974

'He was so money-conscious it was incredible. I worked with him in television and do you know what he did when he bought a drink? He wrote it down on a little pad.'

On Don Revie again 1984

OLD BIG "EAD

'He couldn't keep a clean sheet to save his bloody life.'
On Ron Greenwood at West Ham 2002

'It never ceases to amaze me that so many people have so much difficulty in assembling a good football team. How can they make such a simple job so complex?' 1989

'The manager's office on a Sunday morning when you've lost the day before is a very lonely place.' 1990

'I like the look of Mourinho. There's a bit of the young Clough about him.'
On Chelsea's José Mourinho 2004

BRIAN ON PLAYERS

The common argument – perpetuated by
people who didn't know Brian or his methods
– was that he ruled exclusively through fear. '*If
that's the case*,' he'd say, '*why are so many
players willing to play for me, and why do so
many come back to this club* [he meant
Nottingham Forest] *after leaving it?*' There'd
usually be a pause. '*Perhaps they liked my
singing*,' he'd add.

In truth, Brian had a talent, which he
shared with Peter Taylor, for being able to
unravel the psychological DNA of players.
Clough's basic philosophy was, simply put:
'*You have to get players relaxed because in
any profession you do better when you're not
afraid ... You can't do that if you rule by fear*.'
Mind you, this was the same manager who
defended striking Roy Keane with the words:
'*I only ever hit Roy the once. He got up, so I
couldn't have hit him very hard*'; and

OLD BIG 'EAD

dismissed the talents of David Beckham (and his wife Victoria) with the put-down: '*His wife can't sing and his barber can't cut hair.*' Woe betide any player who disagreed with him. '*There are never any disagreements with players,*' he said. '*We talk about it for twenty minutes and then we decide I was right.*' He wasn't joking.

'I used to talk a lot to a man named Harry Storer and he used to say that players had no bloody brains at all.'

On the advice he was given by one of his mentors 1981

'Me? Rely on footballers? That's crap. If I relied on footballers, I would have been out of a job 20 years ago.' 1983

'The only thing that doesn't move on a football pitch is the posts.'

Advice to strikers to always hit the target 2001

'I try to be truthful about myself and I think the only way to get the best out of footballers, out of anyone, is to start with the truth. You point out everything that life has to offer and every single thing they might want to run away from. All of us have certain areas of our lives that we're uncomfortable with and we're not too happy to discuss.' 1979

OLD BIG "EAD

'They apply themselves off the field perfectly with their big houses, fast cars, business agents and picking up their fat wage packets – but some of them seem to have forgotten that they can do all that only because of football.' 1980

'If any footballer is under the illusion that a manager's job is NOT to replace him with someone better, then he hasn't been properly educated.' 1974

'Players aren't treated like gods here. They are flesh and blood, they never stop learning their craft.'
On his philosophy at Nottingham Forest 1979

'Floats like a butterfly and stings like one too.'
On Trevor Brooking 1975

'Sinatra said the written word comes first. The music comes later. In football, the one who picks the player comes first. All the bullshit comes later.'
On picking the right players to sign 1990

'It doesn't matter if players like or dislike you. When they respect you, they play for you.' 1985

'When you learn to play with it, you can have the match ball.'
To Peter Withe, who had just scored four goals for Nottingham Forest against Ipswich 1977

'When you are a goalscorer, the penalty area is sacred ground.' 1968

OLD BIG "EAD

'Goalscorers have the hardest job in football. You don't know how difficult it is to score a goal and keep scoring.' 1967

'Stand up straight, get your shoulders back and get your hair cut.'
His first words to John McGovern at Hartlepool 1965

'I've bought him to teach the others how to play.'
On signing John McGovern for Nottingham Forest 1975

'I wanted two hard bastards at the centre of that defence.'
On pairing Larry Lloyd with Kenny Burns in Forest's Championship and European Cup winning teams 1987

'Archie Gemmill was five-foot nowt but he could out-jump six-foot opponents. He used to scare Peter Osgood to death.' 1991

'Have you ever been hit in the stomach?'

His question to Nigel Jemson – before he hit him in the stomach 1991

'I think he's got a lot of talent. And I've asked our coach driver, if he sees him in the tunnel at Wembley, to try and knock him down.'

On Paul Gascoigne before the 1991 FA Cup final

'If we're not careful, Paul Gascoigne is going to end up like Matt Monro. Dead before we appreciate his talent.' 2002

'He gets more than me. I only get £200 a week. He gets £250.'

On Stuart Pearce 1989

OLD BIG "EAD

'I'd have cut his balls off.'

On Eric Cantona's kung fu kick at a fan 1995

'That Seaman is a handsome young man but he spends too much time looking in his mirror rather than at the ball. You can't keep goal with hair like that.'

On Arsenal's David Seaman 2000

'Oh, I'd have sent him home alright, but I'd have shot him first.'

On Roy Keane leaving the Republic of Ireland's World Cup squad after disagreeing with his manager, Mick McCarthy 2002

'Get out of my sight. If I ever see you again, I'll kill you.'

To Justin Fashanu, who had just pulled out of a match with an injury 45 minutes before kick-off 1983

'When anyone mentions Justin Fashanu to me, I say one thing. I didn't buy him. It had nowt to do with me. The person who did buy him didn't do his job properly.'
A criticism of Peter Taylor 1983

'There are three possibilities. You can leave voluntarily. I can call the police and have you removed. Or you can politely ask me to sit down for a minute to reconsider.'
During one of his rows with Justin Fashanu 1983

'Young man, take your hands out of your pockets.'
Before presenting an award to Trevor Francis 1978

'I'll enlarge what he's got, in all areas. I'll do it by a bit of encouragement, bullying, cajoling, teaching, opening his eyes. Isn't that what we all got at school?'
On signing Trevor Francis for £1m 1979

OLD BIG "EAD

'Our Elizabeth could have put it in.'

On Trevor Francis' winning header in the 1979 European Cup final 1990

'Trevor Francis was like a greyhound, a thoroughbred of a player and as sharp as a button when it came to negotiating a deal for himself. He was cuter than all of them in that respect.' 1983

'He pleased his mum.'

On son Nigel's goal against Luton in the Littlewood's Cup final 1988

'The sins of the father shouldn't be heaped on the shoulders of the son.'

On his fear that Nigel would be criticised unfairly because of him 1986

'I know a bit about centre-forwards because I wasn't a bad one myself. I know if you have the heart and can score goals, you have a chance. Nigel has the heart of a lion and knows where the goal is.' 1985

'Martin O'Neill was like James Joyce. He used words I'd never heard of.' 1988

'What is the point of giving you the ball when there is a genius on the other wing?'
Question to Martin O'Neill about John Robertson 1979

'I could point to Robbo and say: "You were a tramp when I came here, and now you're the best winger in the game."'
On John Robertson 1982

OLD BIG "EAD

'He's a little fat lad. But once you get him to accept it, you can go on to say that he's one of the best deliverers of the ball in the game.'

More on John Robertson 1980

'If I was ever feeling off colour, I only had to sit next to John Robertson in the dressing room. Next to him I looked as handsome as Victor Mature.'

1980

'He never even looked at his right foot when he put his shoe on.'

On John Roberston's preference for his left foot 1990

'He was the Picasso of our game.'

On John Robertson again 1991

'When he learns how to trap a ball and kick it, I'll play him.'

On Gary Megson 1984

'I am as bad a judge of strikers as Walter Winterbottom – he only gave me two caps.' 1983

'I said to him that I didn't think he was good enough for international football. I was just trying to make sure we didn't have a cocky bastard on our hands for the next month.'

Handling Stuart Peace after his England call-up 1987

'He's got bigger dimples than Shirley Temple.'

On Teddy Sheringham 1990

'He was the slowest player in the squad – perhaps due to all those nightclubs he kept telling me he didn't frequent.'

On Teddy Sheringham 2001

OLD BIG 'EAD

'The half time Oxo was better.'

On the first time he saw Garry Birtles play in non-League football 1980

'I'm not saying he's thin and pale, but the maid in our hotel room pulled back the sheets and remade the bed without realising he was still in it.'

On Brian Rice 1984

'He was Derby County ... he was better than Bobby Moore.'

On Dave Mackay 1990

'He is a clown.'

On Polish goalkeeper Jan Tomaszewski before England's critical World Cup qualifier 1973

'He knocked us out of the World Cup. How we didn't win six- or seven-one, I'll never know.'

Reflecting on Tomaszewski's performance after England drew 1-1 in 1973 and failed to qualify for the finals 1990

'He won me the championship. We thought if we scored, we'd win 'cos no one could get the ball past him.'

On Peter Shilton 1988

'If I was Shilton, I'd wait for my chance and punch him straight in the head at the very first opportunity. Any corner or free kick would do – it would be a nice little bit of revenge for what he did to us in Mexico.'

Retaliatory advice to Peter Shilton after the 'Hand of God' goal Diego Maradona scored against England in the 1986 World Cup 1986

'It was like buying a painting, like a Constable or a Turner, that you knew in a year or two's time is going to be worth twice what it cost you.'

On signing Peter Shilton 1988

OLD BIG 'EAD

BRIAN ON DIRECTORS

Often Brian uttered the phrase *'board of directors'* as if it were blasphemy. His regard for the abilities of most directors was low enough to be subterranean, and manifested itself in sharp asides that nearly always – either tacitly or explicitly – focused hard on what he saw as their impediments. His view of the perfect director is encapsulated in two lines: *'The ideal director raises money, manages it and passes it on to me to spend as I see fit. If they don't like what I do with it, they can sack me and get someone else.'* He honestly believed it.

OLD BIG "EAD

'I think the very sight of them brings the game into disrepute.'
His opinion of directors 1973

'Football attracts a certain percentage of nobodies who want to be somebodies at a club.' 1995

'Running a football club gets their photograph on the back pages of newspapers – nowt else would.'
His theory on why people want to become football directors 1983

'They only know where to find the free drink and the free food. If we win, it's: "Oh Brian, lovely to see you." If we lose, it's what a bastard the manager is and lots of muttering behind closed doors.' 1993

'In the days when I had to go for interviews for jobs I was asked questions (by directors) who had no idea of the answers. How can you ascertain the correct answer to something when you know bugger all yourself?' 1990

'An ICI foreman was almost certainly once on the shop floor; a bus inspector once drove a bus. But how many FA officials and club directors have ever been footballers?' 1972

'On occasions he's been known to dress like a Christmas tree. But he doesn't only sing better than the other 91 chairmen, he also talks more sense than 95 per cent of them.'

On Elton John, then chairman of Watford 1984

OLD BIG "EAD

'There's a seven-man board at Derby, and I wouldn't give you tuppence for five of them.' 1973

'Now listen, we're relaxing. So either have a glass of wine or bugger off so we can carry on conserving our nervous energy.'
To a Derby director, who asked whether players drinking before a European Cup tie was the best way to prepare 1973

'He brought in a rule that directors at Derby had to retire at 65. But when the old bastard got to 65 himself, he changed it.'
On Sam Longson 1977

'Even when they sack you, don't go anywhere. Let the bastards go first.' 1990

BRIAN'S FOOTBALL PHILOSOPHY

He abhorred the long ball game, which he regarded as agricultural rather than cultural. From the start of his managerial career, he was concerned with the purity of the passing game. *'People want to see something beautiful,'* he'd say. *'It's our job to make the game easy on the eye. If we don't, no one will enjoy watching us.'*

OLD BIG "EAD

'The ball is your best friend. Love it, caress it.'
His advice to players 1987

'I'd love all of us to play football the way Frank Sinatra sings ... all that richness in the sound and every word perfect.' 1993

'No one who hasn't done it realises how lonely the job is.'
On management without an assistant 1985

'Show me someone who is liked by everyone and I'll show you someone who's got it wrong.'
On the basics of management 1979

'The best coaching lesson of all ... After 90 minutes listening to me yell at everyone, whoever it is knows me better than he's ever done before.'
Why he liked players sitting next to him in the dug out 1989

'If you sort out the small things, the big things won't bother you.'

On why he was such a disciplinarian 1972

'A pianist learns to play the piano by spending hours at the keyboard. A painter learns how to paint by standing at an easel. And a footballer learns how to become more skilful at his job by practising it.'

On the importance of coaching with the ball rather than using blackboard and chalk 1983

'If a player is repeatedly getting booked, then the manager should be fined as well as him. We'd stop bookings overnight if that happened.'

1987

OLD BIG "EAD

'You can split footballers into two categories. There were those who 'can play' and those who 'can't'. You'll be surprised how many people can't tell the difference. Some of them are managers.' 1985

'Eric Morecambe used to say to me that the art of all comedy is timing. The art of management is knowing your own players, and I'm not talking about whether someone has a better right foot than his left or can't head the ball for toffee. I'm talking about really knowing them, knowing what sort of person you've got on your hands ... I can tell, from the moment I see someone in the dressing room, whether he's off colour, had a row with his missus, kicked the cat or doesn't fancy it that particular day. I know who needs lifting. I know who needs to have his arse kicked. I know who needs leaving alone to get on with it.'
On the psychology of coaching 1984

'Players lose you games, not tactics. There's so much crap talked about tactics by people who barely know how to win at dominoes.' 2000

'I'm on the same wavelength as players.'
The secret of his coaching 1980

'I'd want them to tell me: Is it the birds, is it the booze or is it the betting? 'Cos most of us are susceptible to one of those things. If I find out that someone likes a bet, I can watch the size of his wallet. If I find out someone likes to chase women, I can see whether his fly is undone. If someone likes a beer, I'll get close enough to smell his breath in the morning. Now that's management ...'
On the first thing he would ask a new signing 1980

'I'm a manager players generally like because I win them things. No one likes to go through their career without winning a medal.'
On his own abilities 1981

OLD BIG 'EAD

'If a player can't trap a ball and pass it by the time he's in the team, he shouldn't be there in the first place. I told Roy McFarland to go out and get his bloody hair cut. That's coaching at top level.' 1972

'It only takes a minute to score a goal.' 1969

'I don't know anything about art. But I do know that one artist influences another artist, persuades him to paint in the same style or use the same colours. I reckon if I can influence just one manager to look at what I did, and then try to do exactly the same himself, then I'll take it as a compliment. I'll know that I was half-decent at my job.' 1987

'Too many players think they can pull their boots off one day and put on a suit the next. They couldn't be more wrong.'

On moving from the pitch into the manager's office 1982

'I don't have many regrets in life, but if I do have one, it's that I never managed a big club. Can you imagine what I could have done at Old Trafford?' 1988

'Time. Cash. A good chairman. The ability to handle players and being the boss when it's necessary. The rest is all about talent.'

On how to be successful in management 1981

'The only thing I've ever seen catch a ball on its nose from 14 feet in the air was a seal I watched as a kid at Blackpool Tower circus.'

On why he despised the long ball game 1990

OLD BIG "EAD

'My philosophy has always been that if you are going to be a manager – or anything else for that matter – that you might as well be the best one there is. In my book, that has always meant winning the League Championship.' 1983

'Football management means strains, pressures and heart attacks, but a real football man cannot resist it.' 1977

'I want first place. Anyone who would settle for less is crackers.' 1969

'Doing well in football is like childbirth – it doesn't happen overnight.' 1979

'People get mixed up about themselves; they become bad judges of what they have to offer. I try to show them what they are really capable of and help them to give it.' 1979

'Never do what they expect you to do, otherwise they'll take you for granted.'
On dealing with players 1985

'The day I tell the chairman that I'm quitting, he'd better grab the keys of the company car, clear my office and take my name off the headed notepaper as soon as the words leave my mouth.'
His belief that people who say they want to quit a job should go – immediately 1986

'One of the worst crimes you can commit, not just in football but in life, is to ask people to deliver something they haven't got. That destroys them totally.' 1979

OLD BIG "EAD

'You can take your League Cups, FA Cups and
European Cups and put them all in a corner. To win
our League Championship is incredible ...'
On the importance of the League Championship 1980

'All great sides are based on clean sheets ... I built
every side I ever managed on them.' 1969

'I lived by the rule that in the first three months of a
manager's life you are at your strongest. Get all the
unpleasant stuff out of the way.' 1990

'Firing people isn't hard.' 1978

'It's a fact of life. It's harder to hang on to success than
to get it.' 1990

BRIAN ON HIMSELF

As well as the bragging and the bombast, Brian frequently expressed a self-deprecating humour – often because it took the pressure off his players. He'd say he had '*shot it*' or that his dog Del Boy '*picked the team*' and he took no part in it. In reality, he was a complicated figure and in certain circumstances not as self-assured as he seemed. He also confessed that in being so outspoken, he had often been his worst enemy. '*At one time people said I talked too much, and they were right – smack on. They said I was unbelievably rude, and they were smack on about that too.*'

OLD BIG "EAD

'I think on occasions I have been big-headed. But I call myself Big Head to remind myself not to be.' 1990

'I didn't set out to create an image. It was just me. You get what you see with me. And you get what you hear.' 2000

'I'm not too proud of being rude. I've been rude since I was 20 years old. I don't mean to be, and it's a thing I should work on and attempt to change.' 1972

'I allow the competitive to overrule the enjoyment. When I play cards for threepence, I play to win. If I play dominoes, I've got to win.' 1972

'Me.'

After being asked about the biggest influence on his career
1983

'I'm a big head, not a figurehead.'
On why he couldn't succeed in the boardroom or in business
1987

'I fear many things. I fear the dark. I fear being out of work. I fear being a failure. I think I fear loneliness the most.' 1972

'If I wanted to do something, I did it – whether it was right or wrong. I always thought I was right.' 2000

'If I'd been an MP, I'd have wanted to be the Speaker. No one else was having the last word.' 1985

'Character. And I've got it.'
The secret of management 1966

OLD BIG "EAD

'I received a Get Well telegram from someone which read: "Didn't know you had one."'
After suspected heart trouble 1982

'There I was in the coronary unit, being wired up like a Christmas tree, but feeling as useful as a Christmas cracker.'
On being in hospital 1982

'I'm fat, fifty and worn out.' 1985

'I would have had problems with foreign players because they wouldn't have been able to understand me ... and I certainly can't speak half of their languages.' 2000

'If the FA [officials] received one quarter of the criticism in one month that I receive in one day, they would want to change jobs.' 1973

'When my kids attempt to take the mickey out of me by asking me to produce my O and A Levels, I run upstairs, grab my medals and bang them down on the table. And then I tell them: "They're the O Levels in my industry."' 1989

'It doesn't give me pleasure, you know – league football. I can't remember many first team games in 25 years that I've actually enjoyed.' 1990

'Sometimes, during a match, especially if things are not going too well, I can't hear myself shout for the pounding in my heart ... During those 90 minutes in the dug-out I die a thousand deaths.' 1990

'I've stayed in it because it's my job and it's the only thing I know. Can't do 'owt else. Too old now to sweep the streets.' 1990

OLD BIG "EAD

'I still love my job. I like getting out in the fresh air. It's the only thing I know how to do.' 1991

'I walked in at night behaving like a football manager and I'd watch my three bairns sitting around thinking: "What is it tonight?" And: "God help us if it's a bad result."' 1977

'Barbara says to me repeatedly: "I don't care what you do at the ground. When you come into the house try and smile."' 1990

'When I get home, get out of my working clothes, put my slippers on and the telly off ... That's the nearest I get to a feeling of perfect peace.' 1989

'No wife can have had a more wretched husband. I must have been terrible to live with.'

On his marriage 1968

'I'd say 95 per cent of football managers take their problems home. I've done it for twenty-odd years. My wife and children have done well to survive.' 1990

'My wife says it stands for Old Big 'Ead.'

On being awarded the OBE in 1991

'I keep imagining arriving at a ground somewhere and the commissionaire saying: "I know you're Brian Clough. But you're not a manager any more pal, and if you don't have a proper ticket you're not coming in."'

Confessing a 'nightmare' that he says stopped him from going to matches after his retirement 1993

OLD BIG 'EAD

'Some people thought me to be a bully but I never meant to be. Possibly it's the way I talk.' 1993

'They laugh when I am being serious.'
On the way people viewed him 1983

'Say nowt. Win something. And then talk your head off.'
Advice to other managers 1972

'I don't know how many great teams a manager can create in a lifetime. Two? Three at most? The thing is, though, you never stop trying. It's like an actor wanting to win another Oscar, a mountaineer who wants another crack at scaling Everest. I'm like that.' 1993

'In this business you have to be a dictator or you haven't got a chance.' 1965

'I would like to be the perfect dicator.' 1971

'If I am nothing else, I am loyal.' 1990

'I am a bit of an idealist. I do believe in fairies.' 1974

'I am a man who holds opinions and uses his platforms to express them. I may not be right every time but I have stimulated the thinking of people in this country.' 1973

'I would dearly have loved to open the batting for Yorkshire.' 1972

'I believe I have been good for football. I do not tell many lies. I am not too big a cheat. And I do not pay lip-service to influential people.' 1972

OLD BIG "EAD

'My terms are simple. If someone wants to employ me they take me as I am.' 1973

'People will tell you that Brian Clough is a young man in too big a hurry. And people are right.' 1968

'I'd give anything for one more season as a player ... If I could turn the clock back, that's what I'd do. I try to tell 'em – every player I get – to enjoy every single minute of their career. 'Cos you never know when it might end, in less than a second. You only have to be unlucky once. Like me.'

On the joy of playing and the injury which ended his own career 1985

'I shout my opinion. I yell my contempt. I mean every word of it. But when you talk like that you are a target. I've got to be a winner or they'll cut me to shreds.' 1972

'People who get into a situation where they have large sums of money often collect things – Georgian silver or rare stamps or paintings. But the money I have will buy me the time to collect nice people around me.' 1972

'I was an absolute fanatic between the ages of 25 and 35, a fanatic who wanted to change the world.'
On his zeal for politics 1981

'Conceit and arrogance are part of a man's make-up. I just had too much.' 1974

'It becomes difficult to remain normal after the life I've led.' 1975

'I love retirement. I love living quietly for once.' 1994

OLD BIG "EAD

'If you don't laugh, you cry.'
Philosophy of life 1980

'After I've been gone for a while, it'll be as if I never existed in football.' 1993

BRIAN ON DRINK AND DRINKING

A drink problem tragically blighted the final few seasons of Brian's managerial career. When he could no longer pretend otherwise, he talked about it with good humour. '*Walk on water? I know most people out there will be saying that instead of walking on it, I should have taken more of it with my drinks. They are absolutely right*.' He had a liver transplant in 2002.

OLD BIG 'EAD

'I went berserk for a time. I drank heavily. I wasn't very manly.'

On his mental state after injury ended his career prematurely
1967

'I just walk around and booze.'

His reply after being asked what he did by someone who didn't know him 1984

'Alcohol.'

When asked to name his favourite drink 1983

'I do not have a problem with drink at all. I am not a boozer. I have a drink in the privacy of my own home – a drop of sherry. I have the occasional glass of wine over lunch. That's it.' 1993

'Sure, I drink a bit too much on occasions but then, doesn't everybody?' 1993

'To put everyone's mind at rest, I'd like to stress that they didn't give me George Best's old liver.'

After his own liver transplant 2003

BRIAN ON BOWING OUT

With relegation in 1993 came his resignation,
and an amalgam of sadness and adulatory
acclaim for Brian's 18 years at Nottingham
Forest. Asked, mid-way through the season,
why Forest were at the bottom of the table, he
replied succinctly and with typical candour:
'We're crap.' The pressures of management,
however, made retirement one of his regular
discussion topics well before he finally quit.

OLD BIG "EAD

'Go home. Sleep on it. If you feel the same way the next morning, take another 24 hours. And then another 24 hours after that. Never resign. I did it once. It was the worst decision I ever made.'

His advice to managers who were contemplating resignation 1982

'I always said I'd be out of football by the time I was 50. Then I found out that 50 arrived quicker than I anticipated.' 1990

'The thing that worries me about retirement is that I'll have to sit with directors and directors' wives who have no idea about football. To sit among that lot and listen to the chatter will be a very hard thing to do.' 1987

'I am staying here until they shoot me because I am finishing after that.'

Asked whether he would move to another League club before retiring 1987

'I can't get the sack. The only way I'm leaving this club is walking out, "quitting" to use one of the scum paper headlines. I ain't going nowhere until I say "yes".'

On being asked about his future mid-way through Forest's relegation season. 1993

'I don't want to leave with the indignity, humiliation and pain that goes with losing your job.'

Insisting he would fight on

'Retirement is something I've been thinking about for nine months but like a woman I might use my prerogative and change my mind.'

Announcing his retirement

OLD BIG "EAD

'She looked at me and said: "If you are not prepared to go, then I'll drag you there by your hair".'

The reply his wife Barbara gave when he told her that he might 'duck' his final home match against Sheffield United

'No disrespect to Dave Bassett ... but I've just been relegated 'cos we've been pissed on by a team who can't particularly play.'

After the defeat against Sheffield United that sent Forest down

'After the last match, I'll be cutting my ties completely. It's a joint decision between me and my wife Barbara.'

Dismissing the idea that he might become Forest's President or join the board.

'If I went back to the City Ground, I fear I might become a bit of an embarrassment. I know what it is like to follow a manager who was entrenched at one club ... If I joined the board whoever took over would feel like a husband with his mother-in-law in the spare bedroom.'

Explaining why he preferred to stay away

'Easy to be cross. Easy to be dissatisfied. That's what you get for looking back. No point – it's over.'

On whether he had any regrets about retirement

'I don't know what I'll be doing on Saturday afternoons from now on. But I'll be enjoying myself. Now you lot get out and enjoy yourselves in the second half.'

His final half-time team talk – against Ipswich at Portman Road

'I have a feeling that, over the season, the manager wasn't good enough either.'

On taking his share of the blame for relegation

OLD BIG "EAD

'I've had enough and I'm getting out to enjoy what's left of my life.'
On bowing out

'I hope, when I've gone, people will say I did it right. I played football on the grass.'
On posterity

BRIAN SHOOTING FROM THE LIP

On TV, Brian once rebuked an interviewer with the argument: '*You ask me questions you wouldn't dare ask anyone else.*' He was right. But Brian also knew it was because he was likely to provide more stimulating answers. He became his own Dictionary of Quotations.

OLD BIG "EAD

'Shithouse is an affectionate term at this club.'

Explaining why he often used the word rather than a person's name

'True fame is when the newspapers spell your name right in Karachi.' 1980

'I found that the only people who aren't obsessed with money are those who have got more than enough of it.' 1979

'It's Mr Clough to you.'

In response to anyone he didn't know calling him Brian

'Call me Brian.'

In response to anyone he didn't know calling him Mr Clough

'Hey, get a fag on. I like to smoke by proxy.'

Regular order to the Forest coach driver during away trips

'To allow live football is the worst decision I've heard in years. I don't see how the public will pay good money to watch the game when they can sit at home and see one for nothing ... I stick to my view that showing football live on TV will kill the game stone dead within three years.' 1983

'If you took a cross section of the public, or any particular profession, I don't think you'd find so many dishonest men per thousand.'

On Members of Parliament 1974

'If the BBC ran a Crap Decision of the Month competition on *Match of the Day*, I'd walk it.'

Chastising himself 1993

OLD BIG "EAD

'I'm convinced that some people in London still think anyone north of the M25 lives in a cave, wears a flat cap and goes whippet racing.' 1988

'They say that Rome wasn't built in a day, but I wasn't on that particular job.' 1998

'I'm always me – the man who says the right thing at the wrong time.' 1978

'How is it that we can't get everyone in work with talent? We've got enough shithouses in work without talent.'
Political speech 1988

'He's already taken over my office and the team talk. Now I've taught him to stop eating the carpet at home, he'll learn how to pick the team.'
On his dog Del Boy 1988

'Women run everything. The only thing I've done in my house for twenty years is recognise Angola as an independent state.' 1997

'Bloody driver got lost. Hey, I reckon his last job was driving Rommel's staff car.'
Explaining to the media why he was late for a press conference in Cologne 1979

'There is no such thing as a football hooligan. They are just hooligans. Football hooligans? Well, there are 92 club chairman for a start. There are more hooligans in the House of Commons than at a football match.' 1985

'The next time I lead my team to Wembley, I don't want to see Margaret Thatcher sitting there.'
On his opposition to membership cards 1985

'You get membership cards at local libraries. As far as football is concerned it is so idiotic it should have dropped out of a Christmas cracker.'
And again 1985

OLD BIG 'EAD

'Our beloved Prime Minister and I do have one thing in common. We're the only two people who could resign right now and get a cheer of thanks capable of drowning out Big Ben.'
Comparing his popularity to Margaret Thatcher's 1988

'The only thing she hasn't outlawed is voting Labour.'
On Margaret Thatcher 1983

'Pay off your mortgage as soon as you can. The banks rob you blind.' 1982

'A woman asked me what I was doing over Christmas. I told her I was working. We've got about 50 matches in the next 10 days. If Santa Claus had that sort of workload, he wouldn't finish delivering the presents until Spring Bank Holiday. We play too many matches in this country – it's crackers.' 1987

'My socialism comes from the heart. I've been lucky. I've got a few bob in the bank, a nice house, a nice car and nice things around me. I see no reason on earth why everyone can't have what I've got.' 1968

'When people ask me how I'm doing, I always give them the same answer: "I'm surviving."' 1984

'The pigeons in Derby will welcome the news. There'll be more room on my head to shit on than anyone else's.'
On plans to erect a statue in his honour in Derby 2002

'When I go, God's going to have to give up his favourite chair.' 2000

CODA

Brian Clough died of stomach cancer in Derby on 20 September 2004. He once said: '*Don't send me flowers when I'm dead. If you like me, send them while I'm alive.*' Asked how he'd like to be remembered, he remarked: '*I want no epitaphs of profound history and all that type of thing. I contributed – I hope they will say that, and I would hope somebody liked me.*'

We did, Brian.

OLD BIG "EAD